ALLERGYCOOKIE
Top 8 free. Fun for kids. Easy for moms.

52 ALLERGY Friendly COOKIES for KIDS

By Tiffany Rogers

www.allergycookie.com

LAYOUT DESIGN BY LYNNE BURNS

CHARACTER ART BY JAMES ROGERS

Find More Info on the Web!

 ALLERGY COOKIE YOU TUBE CHANNEL
https://www.youtube.com/allergycookie

 ALLERGY COOKIE PINBOARDS
(featuring top 8 free products, cookbooks, recipe sites, etc.)
https://www.pinterest.com/allergycookie/

 KITCHEN SCIENCE TIPS
https://www.allergycookie.com/kitchen-science-101/

 DOWNLOAD THE INTERACTIVE PDF EBOOK FOR 75% OFF
(Use Code COOKIE75)
https://www.allergycookie.com/product/52cookies/

Welcome!

There's no better way to get excited about creating in the kitchen than by baking up our simple and sweet top 8 allergen free cookies! Plus, you have the added benefit of delicious joy that comes from a fresh baked cookie you know has been prepared in a safe place.

No eggs or milk in the batter means even kids who aren't allergic can still safely sample the batter (who doesn't like licking the spoon?). Plus, we have options for your vegan friends too.

These recipes also work great for wheat eating friends. If you can safely eat wheat in your house, just substitute the gluten free flour for wheat flour in most of these recipes and your cookies will still be delicious!

Don't forget to read our important Cookie Tips *(see page 4)* before you get started. We hope you have a fun and safe time creating these sweet treats!

ALLERGYcookie
Top 8 free. Fun for kids. Easy for moms.

IN THIS BOOK

Chef Cookie Tips

Hey kids! I'm Chef Cookie, here to tell you some important things to remember when making cookies from this book! Make sure you read all of my tips before you get started and watch for more along the way. Stay safe and have fun!

TIP #1: SAFETY FIRST

None of the foods in this book contain any of the top 8 food allergens, but that doesn't mean they are safe for you! Check with your parents about each food (some might be made on shared lines or have other ingredients your parents want you to avoid).

TIP #2: USE OUR PINBOARDS

Don't forget to checkout the Allergy Cookie Pinboards for more ideas on great top 8 free ingredients and decorating candies!

TIP #3: ICING AND FROSTING ARE NOT THE SAME

Royal icing is great for decorating and works well in condiment bottles or decorator bags because it dries firm and shiny, but sometimes you want the flavor and texture of a frosting! Pay attention to the type of icing or frosting recommended for each cookie, but don't be afraid to experiment and mix it up either.

TIP #4: ASK A PARENT FOR HELP

Always remember to have a parent help you with the stove, oven and hard places to reach in the kitchen!

Icing and Frosting Recipes

There are so many ways to make icing and frosting! You can have different textures, consistency, flavors and colors, depending on what you want to do with it. In this book, we'll use three different recipes to get you started and even tell you which one we like best for each cookie in our book... but don't stop there!

Put your creativity to work by mixing and matching as you wish! You can find even more recipes on our site.

ROYAL ICING

This icing is great for decorating because is dries firm and fast. We use it for building cookie houses during the holidays but it also works great for dipping cookies to get frosting all the way to the edges of tricky shapes or any other time you want the frosted surface to be smooth and shiny.

Chef Cookie Tip:

Work quickly with this icing and keep the portion you aren't using covered with a wet cloth to keep it from getting too firm, too quick. If it does harden up before you're done with it, you can always microwave it for a few seconds or even run your fingers under warm water, then use your wet fingers to shape the icing how you like it!

What You Need

1/4 c. warm water

1 T. light corn syrup

3 c. powdered sugar

safe food coloring
(optional)

What To Do

1. Mix warm water and corn syrup until corn syrup is dissolved.

2. Gradually add powdered sugar, stirring, until well blended.

3. Beat on high 7 to 10 minutes, until glossy.

4. Add food coloring, if desired.

BUTTERCREAM FROSTING

This is the type of frosting that you put on cakes. It's thick, rich buttery flavor is a delicious way to frost any cookie with a creamy look without any decorating required. Of course, you can always add sprinkles or candies as you wish!

What You Need

2 3/4 c. powdered sugar

1/4 c. safe butter alternative

1 t. vanilla extract

2 T. safe milk alternative

boiling hot water (1 t. at a time)

What To Do

1. Blend powdered sugar with butter alternative (mixture will be dry and crumbly, not smooth).

2. Beat in milk substitute and vanilla.

3. Add small amounts of hot water until you achieve the consistency you want.

CREAM "CHEEZE" FROSTING

Some cookies just don't taste the same without this amazing frosting... especially the cookies that we top with real, fresh fruit. Enough said, go ahead and try it for yourself!

What You Need

4 oz. cream cheese alternative

2 T. safe butter alternative

1 c. powdered sugar

What To Do

1. Cream together butter alternative and cream cheese alternative.

2. Add powdered sugar until well blended.

3. Whip to desired consistency.

Anytime Cookies

You don't need a season or special occasion to make these cookies. They are great to make (and eat) any time or for any reason!

CHOCOLATE CHIP COOKIES

What You Need

2/3 c. safe butter alternative

1/2 c. sugar

1/2 c. packed brown sugar

1 t. vanilla

1 1/2 c. gluten free baking flour

1 T. fruit pectin

1/2 t. soda

1/2 t. salt

2 to 4 T. milk alternative

6 oz. (1 1/4 cups) safe chocolate chips

10

What To Do

1. Have a grown up help you preheat the oven to 375 degrees F.

2. Mix together dry ingredients (except chocolate chips) and set aside.

3. Cream butter alternative and sugars.

4. Add vanilla.

5. Add dry ingredients.

6. Add milk, 1 tablespoon at a time until dough is sticky, but manageable.

7. Gently fold in chocolate chips.

8. Roll into balls and chill in fridge 1 to 2 hours or in freezer for 15 minutes.

9. Bake at 375 F for 8 to 10 minutes.

10. Let cool 10 minutes on cookie sheet.

11. Remove to wire rack.

Chef Cookie Tip:

Sometimes gluten free dough batter can be a little sticky, but that's ok! The sticky dough means your cookie will still be soft after it's baked. If your dough is too sticky to work with, chill it in the freezer for 15 to 20 minutes (don't add more flour). You should be able to work with the dough much easier once it has been chilled. As you handle the dough, it will get warmer so don't forget to chill it again after it's shaped into balls!

Chef Cookie Tip:

You can make your own oat flour by grinding old fashoned oats in your food processor! (about 1 1/2 cups oats will make 1 cup flour)

OATMEAL RAISIN COOKIES

What You Need

1 c. safe butter alternative

1 c. brown sugar

1/4 c. sugar

1/4 c. apple sauce

1-2 T. safe milk alternative

1 T. vanilla

1 T. molasses

1 1/2 c. oat flour

1 t. baking soda

1 1/2 t. ground cinnamon

1/2 t. salt

3 c. old fashioned rolled oats

1 c. raisins

12

What To Do

1. Have a grownup help you pre-heat the oven to 350 degrees F.

2. In a large mixing bowl, cream butter alternative and sugars.

3. Stir in milk alternative, vanilla, & molasses.

4. In a separate bowl, mix together dry ingredients (except raisins and oats).

5. Add dry ingredients to wet mixture and blend well.

6. Stir in raisins & oats.

7. Shape dough into balls and chill in the freezer for 15 minutes or the fridge for 30 to 60 minutes.

8. Bake at 350 for 10 minutes.

9. Let cookies cool for 5 minutes on cookie sheet before moving to a cooling rack.

Chef Cookie Tip:

Don't forget to chill your dough before shaping into balls if it's too sticky to handle (see page 11).

One cookie baking problem that seems to happen a lot occurs when the last batch is in the oven.

Can you guess what that is? Yep, you got it! while you're busy cleaning up, you forget about the cookies still baking and they get burnt! Don't let that happen to yours ... set the timer for every batch, even if you feel like you're a pro!

SOFT SUGAR COOKIES

What You Need

4 3/4 c. gluten free baking flour

1 T. + 1 t. baking powder

3/4 t. baking soda

2 T. fruit pectin

1/2 t. salt

1 c. safe butter alternative

1 1/2 c. sugar

4 to 6 oz. safe yogurt

1/4 c. safe milk alternative

2 T. apple cider vinegar

1 t. vanilla

14

What To Do

1. Have a grown up help you preheat the oven to 375 degrees F.

2. Mix dry ingredients and set aside.

3. Cream butter alternative and sugar.

4. Add yogurt alternative, milk alternative, apple cider vinegar, and vanilla.

5. Using a paddle or dough hook, slowly add dry ingredients.

6. Mix on low speed until well blended.

7. Roll into ball, wrap in plastic wrap, and refrigerate 30 to 60 minutes (or place in freezer for 15 minutes).

8. On a lightly floured surface, roll out a portion of dough until it's the thickness you like (about 1/8 to 1/4 inch thick).

9. Using cookie cutters, cut into shapes and place on a greased cookie sheet.

10. Bake at 375 for 8 to 10 minutes.

11. Remove from pan and cool completely on cooling rack.

12. Frost and serve same day or flash freeze until ready to use.

Chef Cookie Tip:

Greek style yogurt is thicker than other yogurts so use a full 6 ounces of greek style or 4 ounces of other yogurt in this recipe.

15

Chef Cookie Tip:

Don't forget to chill your dough before shaping into balls if it's too sticky to handle (see page 11).

SNICKERDOODLES

What You Need

1/2 c. safe butter alternative

1/2 c. sugar

1/3 c. brown sugar

1 t. vanilla

1 T. + 2 t. safe milk alternative

1 1/2 c. gluten free baking flour

1 T. fruit pectin

1/2 t. baking soda

1/4 t. cream of tartar

1/4 t. salt

For the sugar cinnamon coating:

1/4 c. sugar

2 t. cinnamon

What To Do

1. Have a grown up help you preheat the oven to 350 degrees F.

2. Mix dry ingredients and set aside.

3. Cream butter alternative & sugar.

4. Add vanilla.

5. Stir half of the dry ingredients into the wet mixture.

6. Add milk alternative.

7. Stir in the rest of the dry ingredients.

8. Chill dough for 15 minutes in the freezer or 30 to 60 minutes in the fridge.

9. Roll dough into balls, then roll balls in the cinnamon sugar mixture and place on a prepared cookie sheet.

10. Using your hand or a the bottom of a cup, slightly flatten each cookie.

11. Bake at 350 for 9 minutes.

12. Let cool 10 minutes on pan before removing to cooling rack.

PUMPKIN CHOCOLATE CHIP COOKIES

What You Need

1 c. canned pumpkin

1/2 c. oil

1 c. sugar

2 c. gluten free baking flour

2 t. baking powder

1 t. baking soda

1 1/2 t. cinnamon

1/2 t. salt

1 t. safe milk alternative

1 T. vanilla

11 oz. safe chocolate chips

18

What To Do

1. Have a grown up help you preheat the oven to 350 degrees F.

2. Mix dry ingredients (except chocolate chips) and set aside.

3. In a large mixing bowl combine pumpkin, oil, and sugar.

4. Add milk alternative and vanilla to wet ingredients.

5. Add dry ingredients and mix until well combined.

6. Fold in chocolate chips.

7. Drop cookies on by the spoonful onto a prepared cookie sheet.

8. Bake at 350 for 10-12 minutes.

9. Cool on pan for 10 minutes before removing to cooling rack.

Have you ever snuck back into the kitchen after baking cookies and snatched an extra cookie from the cookie jar when you thought nobody was looking?

Guess what?! They know! Call it a super sense that your parents have, but they always seem to know when someone is sneaking cookies (even if they don't call you out on it) so you may as well fess up and tell the truth!

FLOURLESS SUNBUTTER COOKIES

What You Need

1 c. sunflower seed butter or other nut butter alternative

1 c. sugar

1 small ripe banana

1 T. vanilla

1 1/2 T. safe milk alternative

Chef Cookie Tip:
Have fun experimenting with different types of nut butter alternatives, including both crunchy and creamy varieties! They all work great in this recipe!

What To Do

1. Have a grown up help you preheat the oven to 350 degrees F.

2. Peel banana and smash into a mushy texture with a fork.

3. In a large mixing bowl, cream together sunflower seed butter, sugar, and banana.

4. Add vanilla and safe milk alternative.

5. Form dough into balls and place on a prepared cookie sheet.

6. Using a fork, press each cookie flat.

7. Bake at 350 for 10 to 12 minutes.

8. Cool on pan for 2 minutes before removing to cooling rack.

Want to know the secret behind making these cookies work?

The sunbutter replaces the butter in normal cookies and the banana replaces eggs or other binders. Once you learn the science, there's so many creative ways to substitute ingredients and make super creative cookie recipes of your own!

SUNBUTTER AND JELLY THUMBPRINTS

What You Need

1 c. sunflower seed butter or other nut butter alternative

1 c. sugar

1 small ripe banana

1 T. vanilla

1 1/2 T. safe milk alternative

Your favorite jam or jelly

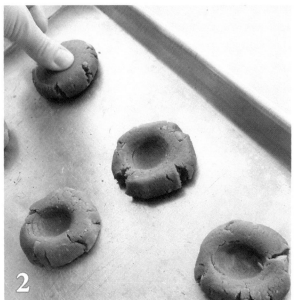

What To Do

1. Have a grown up help you pre-heat the oven to 350 degrees F.

2. Peel banana and smash into a mushy texture with a fork.

3. In a large mixing bowl, cream together sunflower seed butter, sugar, and banana.

4. Add vanilla and safe milk alternative.

5. Form dough into balls and place on a prepared cookie sheet.

6. Using the bottom of a cup, press each cookie flat. *(Fig. 1)*

7. Using your thumb or a small spoon, press the center of each cookie to create a bowl shape in the center. *(Fig. 2)*

8. Fill each with your favorite jam or jelly. *(Fig. 3)*

9. Bake at 350 for 10 to 12 minutes.

10. Cool on pan for 2 minutes before removing to cooling rack.

LUAU COOKIES

What You Need

1 c. safe butter alternative

3/4 c. packed brown sugar

1/2 c. sugar

3/4 t. vanilla

2 1/2 c. gluten free flour blend

1 T. fruit pectin

1 t. baking soda

1/2 t. salt

1 c. coconut

1/2 c. craisins

3/4 c. finely chopped dried mango

3/4 c. orange juice

What To Do

1. Have a grown up help you pre-heat the oven to 325 degrees F.

2. In a medium-sized bowl, mix together flour, pectin, soda, & salt.

3. In a separate bowl, cream butter alternative and sugars.

4. Add vanilla.

5. Stir in flour mixture until well combined.

6. Fold in coconut, craisins, & mango.

7. Add juice gradually, while stirring, until the dough is the consistency you like.

8. Drop spoonfuls onto greased cookie sheets.

9. Bake at 325 for 10 - 12 minutes.

10. Cool on pans for 10 minutes before removing to wire rack.

Did you know that just about any kind of liquid can replace another liquid in a cookie recipe?

We used orange juice instead of milk in these luau cookies, but how would they would taste with cranberry juice or apple juice? What about your favorite flavor of soda, milk alternative, or water? Don't be afraid to experiment with different liquids in your cookie recipes and have fun creating!

CLASSIC NO-BAKE COOKIES

What You Need

1 c. sugar

1 1/2 T. cocoa

1/4 c. safe butter alternative

1/4 c. safe milk alternative

1/2 t. vanilla

1/3 c. sunflower seed butter or other nut butter alternative

1 1/2 c. quinoa flakes

Chef Cookie Tip:

This recipe involves cooking over the stove so be sure to have an adult help you at all times and stay safe!

What To Do

1. In a small saucepan, mix sugar & cocoa.

2. Add butter and milk alternatives, stirring over medium heat until dissolved.

3. Boil for 2 minutes.

4. Remove from heat.

5. Add sunflower seed butter, quinoa, & vanilla.

6. Drop onto wax paper.

7. Allow to cool completely before eating.

Do you have any special cookie making traditions in your family?

We have a special no-bake cookie pot that has been used to make no-bake cookies for multiple generations and even have a designated official no-bake cookie taste tester!

COOKIE DOUGH TRUFFLE POPS

What You Need

Chocolate Chip Cookie Dough, raw *(see page 10)*

Safe chocolate of your choice

Royal Icing *(see page 6)*

Decorative straws or sucker sticks

Chef Cookie Tip:

Don't forget to chill your cookie dough before making these truffle pops so it will stick to itself instead of your fingers (see page 11)!

28

Chef Cookie Tip:

Try putting the royal icing in a decorator bag or condiment bottle and making all kinds of fun designs on these cookie pops!

What To Do

1. Shape cookie dough into balls and place on lined cookie sheet.

2. Insert one straw or sucker stick into each cookie dough ball.

3. Chill in freezer for 15 minutes.

4. While dough is chilling, melt chocolate pieces in the microwave by warming for 30 seconds, stirring, microwaving again for 30 seconds, and continuing to repeat this process until the chocolate is evenly melted and smooth.

5. Remove cookie dough from freezer and roll in chocolate until evenly coated.

6. Return to wax paper and chill in freezer for another 15 minutes.

7. Remove from freezer and drizzle royal icing over cookie pops.

8. Let icing dry and firm completely before serving.

These are so fun and easy to make and will be a hit at any party.

Even the adults will say they melt in their mouths!

SPORTS BALL COOKIE POPS

What You Need

Soft cookies of your choice

Royal Icing *(see page 6)*

Decorative straws or sucker sticks

Sprinkles *(optional)*

Safe food coloring

Chef Cookie Tip:

Try finding a simple picture of the ball you are creating and have it available to look at while you are decorating each cookie!

What To Do

1. Decide which types of balls you want to make and determine the colors you will need for each.

2. Divide your icing into separate bowls and use safe food coloring to create all of the colors you will need.

3. Insert one straw or cookie stick into each cookie.

4. Frost each cookie with the base color of the ball you are creating and let sit for a few minutes to firm up.

5. Using a condiment bottle or decorator bag, create the ball design on the cookie.

6. Let sit to firm completely before serving.

For a football field:

Dip the top third of the cookie in safe sprinkles while the icing is still moist to represent the crowd of people, then use royal icing to draw the yard lines.

For a golf ball:

Try using the end of a sucker stick to create texture in the icing while it is still moist, then let sit to firm up.

These balls are so fun!

They can easily be made with store bought cookies and you can design just about any type of ball you can think of. In addition to the pops shown in the picture, try soccerballs, tennis balls, volleyballs or even golf balls.

FISHBOWL COOKIES

What You Need

Fresh baked or store bought cookies

Buttercream Frosting *(see page 7)*

Fish shaped candies *(safe for you)*

Food decorator pearls
(safe for you)

Safe food coloring

Chef Cookie Tip:

Candy decors like the pearls in this recipe are changing all the time. Check the cake decorating aisle the next time you're out shopping to discover new options that are safe for you!

32

What To Do

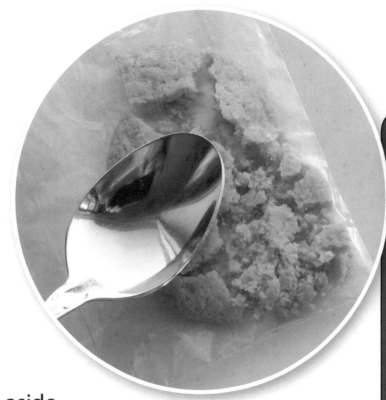

1. Before you get started, prepare cookie crumbs by placing one cookie inside of a sealed sandwich bag and tapping gently with a spoon until the cookie crumbles.

2. Set your cookie crumbs aside and use safe food coloring to create blue frosting.

3. Frost each cookie with the blue frosting.

4. Sprinkle a few cookie crumbs on the bottom of each cookie to create sand.

5. Add fish candy and pearls.

Chef Cookie Tip:

If you can't find fish-shaped candies that are safe, you can make your own using royal icing and wax paper! Simply use the icing to draw your fish on wax paper and wait for them to dry and firm up (possibly overnight).Then, carfully peel them away from the wax paper and place them on your cookies!

PARTY COOKIES

What You Need

Soft sugar cookie dough
(*see page 14*)

Decorator sprinkles (*safe for you*)

These cookies are great for:

▸ birthday parties

▸ new years celebrations

▸ or just anytime you feel like making an easy an easy treat to impress a crowd!

34

What To Do

1. Prepare cookie dough as directed.

2. Fold in sprinkles.

3. If needed, chill the dough in the freezer for 15 minutes, or the fridge for 30 to 60 minutes.

4. Roll dough into balls and place on prepared cookie sheet.

5. Using the bottom of a cup, flatten the cookies to desired thickness.

6. Bake cookies at the same time and temperature recommended in your original sugar cookie recipe.

What's the funnest birthday party you've ever been to?

Where did you go, what did you do, and who was the party for? Don't be surprised if you find that your best birthday party memories are the times you've spent with close friends and family celebrating your own birthdays!

CAMO COOKIES

What You Need

Soft sugar cookie dough
(see page 14)

Food coloring *(safe for you)*

Chef Cookie Tip:

When you're smashing the dough together, be careful not to mix the colors! Start by pressing together three pieces of all different colors, then press three more pieces around the outside of the first three.

 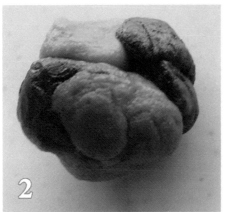

What To Do

1. Prepare cookie dough as directed and chill.

2. Divide dough into three equal pieces and use safe food coloring to color one piece black, another brown, and the last green.

3. Using two small portions of each color of dough, create one ping-pong sized ball by randomly smashing each piece of dough together. *(Fig. 1 & 2)*

4. Place each ball on a on prepared cookie sheet.

5. Using the bottom of a cup, flatten the cookies to desired thickness.

6. Bake cookies at the same time and temperature recommended in your original sugar cookie recipe.

www.allergycookie.com

Try making camo cookies for:

▶ your next Memorial Day barbeque

▶ to celebrate the homecoming of a soldier

▶ or maybe just a fun, army themed birthday party!

37

FOOD ALLERGY AWARENESS COOKIES

What You Need

Soft sugar cookie dough *(see page 14)*

Food coloring *(safe for you)*

Gold sugar sprinkles

Raise awareness for food allergies by making these cookies for your next social event and sharing their story:

▸ Teal = Food Allergy

▸ Magenta = Eosinophilic Disorders

▸ Gray = FPIES

▸ Gold = Loved ones lost to anaphylaxis

What To Do

1. Prepare cookie dough as directed and chill.

2. Divide dough into three equal pieces and use safe food coloring to color one piece teal, another magenta, and the last gray.

3. On a lightly floured surface, roll out each piece of cookie dough until it is about 1/8 to 1/4 inch thick.

4. Carefully lift the magenta cookie dough and place it on top of the teal dough.

5. Next, place the gray dough over top of the magenta. *(Fig. 1)*

6. Starting on one end, roll the dough until you reach the other end (like a cinnamon roll). *(Fig. 2)*

7. Roll in gold sugar sprinkles. *(Fig. 3)*

8. Starting on one end, slice into round cookies and place on prepared cookie sheet. *(Fig. 4)*

9. Bake cookies at the same time and temperature recommended in your original sugar cookie recipe.

Winter Cookies

These cookies are perfect for any winter-themed party or other winter holiday like Valentines and Presidents Day, but not Christmas. We've saved the best for last—there's a whole chapter of Christmas cookies waiting for you at the end of the book! *(See page 109)*

www.allergycookie.com

SNOWMAN PRETZEL COOKIES

What You Need

Safe pretzels (*round shape*)

Royal Icing (*see page 6*)

Safe fruit leather

Safe chocolate chips (*miniature*)

Orange gummy candy

Wax paper

42

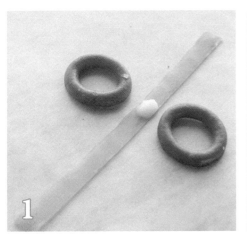
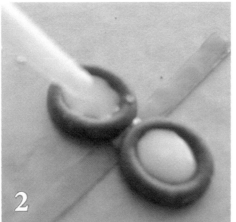
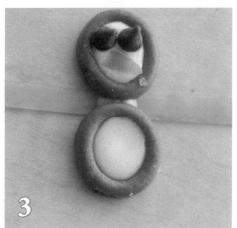
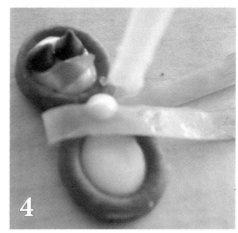

What To Do

1. Slice fruit leather into thin strips (for snowman's scarf) and lay each on wax paper.

2. Using a condiment bottle or decorator bag, place a dot of royal icing in the center of each strip. *(Fig. 1)*

3. Place two pretzels on each strip of fruit leather, so that both touch the dot of icing. *(Fig. 2)*

4. Fill icing in between the two pretzels (to help stick them together) and then fill the center of each pretzel with icing. *(Fig. 2)*

5. Using a table knife, slice gummy candies into small slivers to represent carrot noses.

6. Place the orange candies and chocolate chips on each cookie to create snowman faces. *(Fig. 3)*

7. Fold each scarf up over the pretzels, using royal icing to secure it. *(Fig. 4)*

8. Let cookies sit overnight to dry and firm up before removing them from the wax paper.

SNOWFLAKE COOKIES

What You Need

Fresh baked or store bought cookies

Royal Icing *(see page 6)*

Safe food coloring

Sugar

44

What To Do

1. Use safe food coloring to color about 2/3 of the icing blue.

2. Frost each cookie with blue icing and let sit a few minutes to firm.

3. Meanwhile, put the remaining icing in a decorator bag or condiment bottle.

4. Use the decorator bag or condiment bottle to draw a snowflake shape on the cookie with white icing. *(Fig. 1 & 2)*

5. Carefully sprinkle snowflake with white sugar. Some of the sugar will fall onto the blue icing, but most of it should stick to the white icing which is more wet.

Chef Cookie Tip:

Don't cut too many marshmallows! You only need 4 marshmallow halves per cookie, but you also need 1 full (un-cut) marshmallow for each cookie.

MARSHMALLOW CAP SNOWMAN

What You Need

Fresh baked or store bought cookies

Buttercream Frosting *(see page 7)*

Safe chocolate chips *(miniature)*

Safe chocolate chips *(regular size)*

Miniature marshmallows

Sugar sprinkles *(any color)*

Firm orange candy
(we used a Mike n Ike)

Wax paper

What To Do

1. Before you get started, cut some of the marshmallows in half. *(Fig. 1)*

2. Prepare your candy (carrot nose) by cutting off one end so that it is flat. *(Fig. 2)*

3. Finally, prepare a piece of wax paper, by tracing around one cookie to create a circle, then cut the circle out of the wax paper.

4. Frost each cookie with white frosting.

5. Place the circle piece of wax paper on each frosted cookie, one at a time, leaving 1/3 of the cookie exposed.

6. Sprinkle sugar sprinkles on the exposed portion of the frosted cookie, then carefully remove the wax paper. *(Fig. 3)*

7. Place the marshmallows along the edge of the sugar sprinkles to resemble the fur on the hat (start with one full marshmallow, then place 4 marshmallow halves across the rest of the cookie.

8. Using the candy and chocolate chips, create a snowman face on the rest of the cookie.

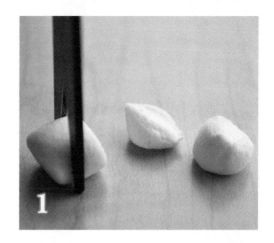

EARMUFF SNOWMAN

What You Need

Fresh baked or store
    bought cookies

Royal Icing *(see page 6)*

Safe fruit ropes

Safe chocolate chips

Firm round candies
    (we used Life Savers)

Firm orange candy
    (we used a Mike n Ike)

What To Do

1. Before you get started, prepare your fruit rope by cutting one third off of the end. *(Fig. 1)*

2. Prepare your candy (carrot nose) by cutting it in half length-wise. *(Fig. 2)*

3. Frost each cookie with white icing.

4. Frost each cookie with white frosting.

5. Create the snowman's earmuffs by curving the fruit rope over the top of the cookie and holding down each end with a round candy.

6. Using the chocolate chips, orange candy, and remaining third of the fruit rope, create a snowman face on the cookie.

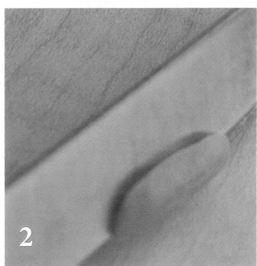

GEORGE WASHINGTON

What You Need

Fresh baked or store bought cookies

Royal Icing *(see page 6)*

Mini marshmallows *(10 per cookie)*

Safe chocolate chips (miniature)

Safe chocolate chips (regular size)

Safe food coloring

One sucker stick

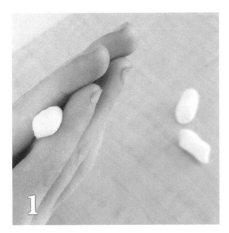   

What To Do

1. Before you get started, prepare 3 marshmallows for each cookie by rolling them between your fingers (lengthwise) to create tube-like shapes. *(Fig. 1)*

2. Dip the end of the sucker stick in food coloring and use it to draw smiling lips on each cookie. *(Fig. 2)*

3. Using royal icing in a condiment bottle or decorator bag, secure two miniature chocolate chips for the eyes, then squeeze a thin layer of icing around the outside of the top half of the cookie for attaching the marshmallows. *(Fig. 3)*

4. Secure the three tube-like marshmallows on the top edge of the cookie, then secure three more marshmallows on each side. *(Fig. 4)*

5. Flatten the 10th marshmallow slightly, then use scissors to make a cut in the bottom center of the marshmallow. *(Fig. 4)*

6. Using royal icing, secure this marshmallow to the bottom of the cookie and add one regular sized chocolate chip to create the neck tie.

ABRAHAM LINCOLN

What You Need

Fresh baked or store bought cookies

Royal Icing *(see page 6)*

Safe candy bar *(we used Enjoy Life)*

Safe chocolate chips *(miniature)*

Safe chocolate chips *(regular size)*

Safe food coloring

One sucker stick

What To Do

1. Before you get started, prepare your chocolate bar by slicing off one end of a rectangular piece. *(Fig. 1 & 2)*

2. Dip the end of the sucker stick in food coloring and use it to draw smiling lips on each cookie. *(Fig. 3)*

3. Using royal icing in a condiment bottle or decorator bag, secure two miniature chocolate chips for the eyes, then squeeze a thin layer of icing around the entire outside of the cookie. *(Fig. 4)*

4. Using additional royal icing, secure the hat to the top of the head, then place regular sized chocolate chips around the rest of the cookie to create the hair and beard. *(Fig. 4)*

VALENTINE COOKIE POPS

What You Need

Soft cookies of your choice

Royal Icing *(see page 6)*

Decorative straws or sucker sticks

Safe food coloring

Small heart-shaped cookie cutter

Wax paper

Chef Cookie Tip:
Try putting the royal icing in a decorator bag or condiment bottle and making all kinds of fun designs on these cookie pops!

54

What To Do

1. Using the bottom of a cup, press each cookie slightly flat so the cookie cutter will fit on it. *(Fig. 1)*

2. Next, cut each cookie into heart shapes. *(Fig. 2)*

3. Insert one straw or cookie stick into the bottom end of each cookie heart and lay flat on wax paper. *(Fig. 3)*

4. Using safe food coloring, divide and color the royal icing into different valentine-themed colors.

5. Drizzle the royal icing onto each cookie heart. *(Fig. 4)*

6. Let sit to dry and firm before removing from wax paper.

VALENTINE SANDWICH COOKIES

What You Need

Soft cookies of your choice

Cream "Cheeze" Frosting (see page 8)

Strawberries

Egg slicer or knife

Small heart-shaped cookie cutter

56

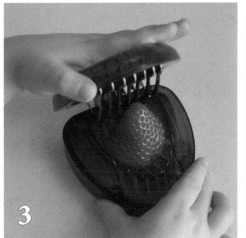

1

2

3

4

What To Do

1. Using the bottom of a cup, press each cookie slightly flat so the cookie cutter will fit on it. *(Fig. 1)*

2. Next, cut each cookie into heart shapes. *(Fig. 2)*

3. Carefully cut the stem out of each strawberry and slice with your egg slicer or knife. *(Fig. 3)*

4. Use the heart-shaped cookie cutter to cut each strawberry into heart shapes. *(Fig. 4)*

5. Using two heart-shaped cookies, one heart-shaped strawberry slice, and some cream 'cheeze' frosting, make little cookie sandwiches for your sweethearts to enjoy!

Chef Cookie Tip:

If your egg slicer has been used for eggs and you're allergic to eggs, you may want to use your own dedicated slicer. Some kitchen specialty stores may even carry slicers that are designed specifically for strawberries.

VALENTINE COOKIE KEBABS

What You Need

Soft cookies of your choice

Creme "Cheeze" Frosting
(*see page 8*)

Strawberries

Heart-shaped strawberry
marshmallows

Small heart-shaped cookie cutter

Decorative straws or skewers

Toothpick

Table knife

What To Do

1. Using the bottom of a cup, press each cookie slightly flat so the cookie cutter will fit on it.

2. Next, cut each cookie into heart shapes.

3. Carefully cut the stem out of each strawberry in a v-shaped pattern, so the strawberry looks like a heart.

4. Cut each strawberry in half to create two heart-shaped strawberries.

5. Using a toothpick, poke a hole in the center of each marshmallow to make it easier to thread.

6. In the pattern of your choice, thread the cookies, marshmallows, and strawberries in your straws or skewers to create kebabs.

CONVERSATION HEART COOKIES

What You Need

Crisp or Crunchy cookies

Royal Icing *(see page 6)*

Safe food coloring

Safe food writer pen

Small heart-shaped cookie cutter

Paper towel

What To Do

1. Prepare your icing by dividing it into portions and using safe food coloring to create the colors you want.

2. Next, moisten a paper towel and squeeze to ring it out.

3. Wrap each cookie (one at a time) in the moist paper towel and microwave for about 20 to 30 seconds until soft.

4. Unwrap the cookie and use the cookie cutter to cut into heart shapes.

5. Frost each cookie with icing and let sit until dry and firm.

6. Write conversation heart messages on each cookie using the food decorator pen.

What are some of the messages you'd like to write on your conversation hearts?

- Best Friends
- Call me
- Thank you
- True Love
- XOXO
- Marry Me

Who would you share your cookies with?

Family, friends, the lonely old lady next door, a secret crush!?! Maybe you'll just eat them yourself! Either way these cookies are fun and easy to create!

MARDI GRAS COOKIES

What You Need

Soft sugar cookie dough
(see page 14)

Food coloring *(safe for you)*

Gold sugar sprinkles

Did you know that Mardi Gras is celebrated in the late winter in New Orleans?

Families enjoy street musicians, artists, and parades put on by a variety of organizations, all leading up to Fat Tuesday, the feast before a 40 day fast called Lent.

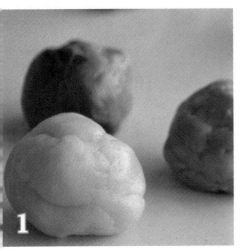 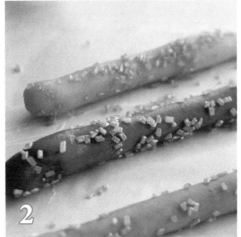 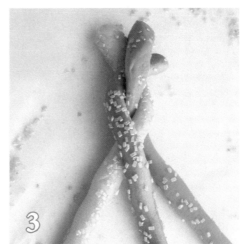 

What To Do

1. Prepare cookie dough as directed and chill.

2. Divide dough into three equal portions and use safe food coloring to color one piece golden yellow, another green, and the last purple.

3. Roll each portion of dough into small balls (a little smaller than ping pong balls). *(Fig. 1)*

4. Next, roll each ball into long, snake-like shapes.

5. Then, roll the snakes in gold sugar sprinkles. *(Fig. 2)*

6. Using one snake of each color, braid the dough. *(Fig. 3)*

7. Finally, roll the braided dough into a round bun and place on a prepared baking sheet. *(Fig. 4)*

8. Bake cookies at the same time and temperature recommended in your original sugar cookie recipe.

64

Spring or Summer Cookies

Flowers, St. Patrick's Day, Easter, and the 4th of July are just a few reasons to celebrate with cookies during the spring and summertime. Have fun!

www.allergycookie.com

Chef Cookie Tip:

If you place a piece of wax paper under the marshmallows before pouring the sprinkles, you can easily bend the wax paper to put the sprinkles back into the bottle. But check with a grown up first. The marshmallows might not be safe for others who will use the sprinkles later, so you it might be better to fold up the wax paper with the sprinkles inside and throw it all away to avoid cross contact.

FLOWER COOKIE POPS

What You Need

Soft cookies of your choice

Buttercream Frosting (*see page 7*)

Decorative straws or sucker sticks

Safe sugar sprinkles

Safe food coloring

Large marshmallows

Toothpicks

Scissors

66

  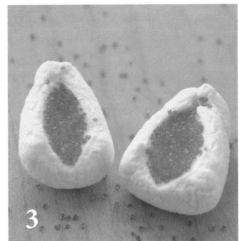 

What To Do

1. Prepare your marshmallows by cutting each in half with a pair of scissors. You will need about 8 halves (4 marshmallows) for each cookie. *(Fig. 1)*

2. Gently squeeze one end of each marshmallow half to create a petal shape. *(Fig. 2)*

3. Pour sprinkles over marshmallows and shake off excess sprinkles (the sprinkles will stick to the inside, sticky portion of the marshmallow all on their own. *(Fig. 3)*

4. Insert one straw or cookie stick into each cookie.

5. Use safe food coloring to create yellow frosting.

6. Frost each cookie with yellow frosting.

7. Using toothpicks, secure each petal to the cookie to create a flower. *(Fig. 4)*

SUGAR CRYSTAL FLOWERS

What You Need

Soft sugar cookie dough
(*see page 14*)

Safe sugar sprinkles

Pastel candies
(*we used Skittles*)

Scissors

What To Do

1. Prepare and chill dough as directed in original recipe.

2. Roll dough into balls, then roll in sugar sprinkles and place on prepared cookie sheet.

3. Using scissors, make three cuts in each ball (like an asterisk).

4. Bake cookies at the same time and temperature recommended in your original sugar cookie recipe.

5. Decorate with pastel candies after decorating.

Chef Cookie Tip:

An easy pattern to follow when making the cuts with your scissors is to first make an X, then cut one straight line through the center of the X.

FLOWER COOKIES

What You Need

Soft sugar cookie dough
(see page 14)

Food coloring
(safe for you)

What To Do

1. Prepare and chill cookie dough as directed.

2. Separate dough into two portions, one being twice the size as the other.

    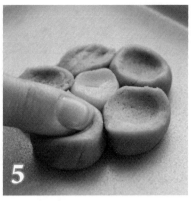

3. Use safe food coloring to color the small portion of dough yellow and the larger portion of dough the color you want your flowers to be.

3. Roll the yellow portion of the dough into a ball.

4. Divide the remaining dough into five equal portions and roll into balls. *(Fig. 1)*

5. Next, roll each ball into long, snake-like shapes (of even lengths). *(Fig. 2)*

6. Surround the yellow snake with the remaining snakes.

7. Gently press the dough into one solid roll, taking care not to squish them out of shape. *(Fig. 3)*

8. Chill the dough in the freezer for 15 to 30 minutes, until firm and difficult to squish.

9. Starting on one end, slice into round cookies and place on prepared cookie sheet. *(Fig. 4)*

10. Using your thumb, gently press the center of each flower petal to create a small dip. *(Fig. 5)*

11. Bake cookies at the same time and temperature recommended in your cookie recipe.

TULIP COOKIES

What You Need

Store bought or fresh
baked cookies

Buttercream Frosting
(see page 7)

Safe fruit ropes

Safe gummy candy
(we used DOTS)

Safe food coloring

Table knife

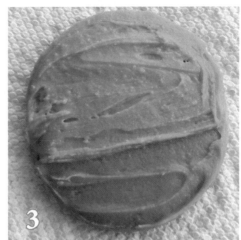

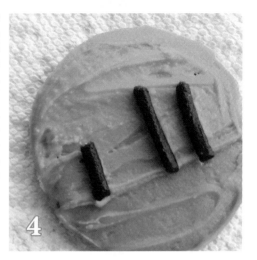

What To Do

1. Prepare gummy candies by using a table knife to cut tulip and leaf shapes. *(Fig. 1 & 2)*

2. Separate frosting and use safe food coloring to create blue and green frosting.

3. Frost the bottom half of each cookie with green frosting and the top half with blue frosting. *(Fig. 3)*

4. Cut the fruit ropes into smaller pieces to create flower stems and place on cookie. *(Fig. 4)*

5. Add tulip shapes and leaves.

POT O' GOLD COOKIES

What You Need

Brown or black cookies

Buttercream Frosting
(see page 7)

Safe fruit ropes

Gold sugar sprinkles

74

What To Do

1. Apply a generous amount of frosting to the top third of the cookie.

2. Place a fruit rope on the cookie to represent the handle, pressing into the frosting at each end until it sticks.

3. Cover frosting with gold sprinkles.

Have you ever tried to catch a leprechaun?

These Pot O' Gold cookies may be just the trick! Set your trap and use the cookies for bait. Check back the next day and remember this: if the cookie is gone and you find a pile of sand in it's place, you've succeeded!

RAINBOW COOKIES

What You Need

Store bought or fresh baked cookies

Buttercream Frosting
(see page 7)

Safe multi-colored candy
(we used Skittles)

Safe black gummy candy
(we used Tootsie Crows)

Safe food coloring

Gold sugar sprinkles

Miniature marshmallows

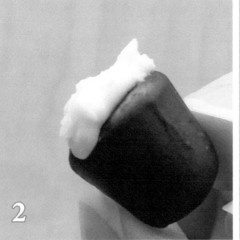
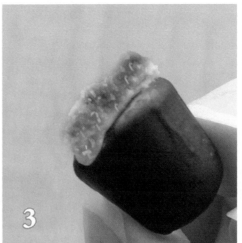

What To Do

1. Separate frosting and use safe food coloring to create blue frosting, leaving a portion of frosting white.

2. Prepare gummy candies and marshmallows by cutting each in half. *(Fig. 1)*

3. Put a small portion of white frosting on the wide end of each black candy, then dip in gold sugar sprinkles to create pots of gold. *(Fig. 2 & 3)*

4. Frost each cookie with blue frosting.

5. In a rainbow pattern, place hard candies on cookie in an arch shape. *(Fig. 4)*

6. Place two marshmallow halves under left side of arch to represent clouds. *(Fig. 4)*

7. Place prepared "pots of gold" under right side of rainbow.

NEST COOKIES

What You Need

Soft cookies of your choice

Coconut

Safe food coloring

Safe jelly beans

Plastic sandwich bag

What To Do

1. Prepare your coconut by placing it in the sandwich bag with a drop or two of green food coloring.

2. Seal the sandwich bag and shake it up until the coconut is green in color. *(Fig. 1)*

3. Using your thumb or a small spoon, press the center of each cookie to create a small nest shape. *(Fig. 2)*

4. Fill each nest with green coconut and jelly beans.

Chef Cookie Tip:

For a more realistic looking (and more natural, healthy to eat) nest, have a grown up help you toast the coconut instead of coloring it green.

EASTER BASKET COOKIES

What You Need

Soft cookies of your choice

Coconut

Safe food coloring

Safe jelly beans

Safe fruit rope

Apple corer

Toothpick

What To Do

1. Prepare your coconut by placing it in the sandwich bag with a drop or two of green food coloring.

2. Seal the sandwich bag and shake it up until the coconut is green in color.

3. Using your thumb or a small spoon, press the center of have of the cookies to create a small bowl shape.

4. Use the apple corer to cut holes in the center of the other half of cookies. *(Fig. 1)*

5. Place one of the cookies with a hole in the center on the top of each of the bowl-shaped cookies. *(Fig. 2)*

6. Using a toothpick, poke two holes in each stack of cookies to make it easier for the fruit rope to fit in. *(Fig. 3)*

7. Insert the fruit rope into each hole to make the basket handle.

8. Fill each basket with coconut and jelly beans. *(Fig. 4)*

JELLY BEAN SURPRISE COOKIES

What You Need

2/3 c. safe butter alternative

1/2 c. sugar

1/2 c. packed brown sugar

1 t. vanilla

1 1/2 c. gluten free baking flour

1 T. fruit pectin

1/2 t. soda

1/2 t. salt

2 to 4 T. milk alternative

6 oz. safe chocolate

Surf Sweets Jelly Beans

82

What To Do

1. Have a grown up help you preheat the oven to 375 degrees F.

2. Mix together dry ingredients (except chocolate chips) and set aside.

3. Cream butter alternative and sugars.

4. Add vanilla.

5. Add dry ingredients.

6. Add milk, 1 tablespoon at a time until dough is sticky, but manageable.

7. Roll into balls and chill in fridge 1 to 2 hours or in freezer for 15 minutes.

8. While dough is chilling, melt chocolate by warming in the microwave 30 seconds at a time, stirring in between.

9. Add jelly beans and stir until well coated. *(Fig. 1)*

10. Remove jelly beans from chocolate and set on wax lined tray. *(Fig. 2)*

11. Place chocolate covered jelly beans in freezer for 15 minutes to cool and set.

12. Gently fold jelly beans into cookie dough, form dough into balls, and place on prepared cookie sheet. *(Fig. 3)*

13. Bake at 375 F for 8 to 10 minutes.

14. Let cool 10 minutes on cookie sheet before removing to cooling rack.

15. Remove to wire rack.

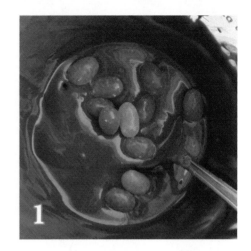

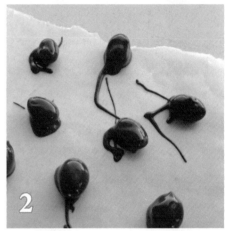

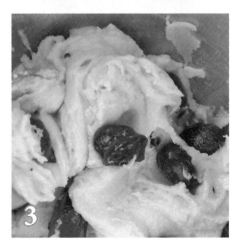

BUNNY COOKIE POPS

What You Need

Soft cookies of your choice

Royal Icing *(see page 6)*

Decorative straws or sucker sticks

Sugar sprinkles

Safe fruit rope

Safe chocolate chips

Large marshmallows

Pink miniature marshmallows

Toothpicks

Table knife

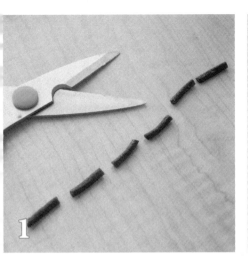

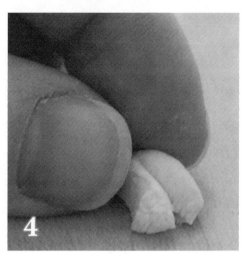

What To Do

1. Prepare the bunny ears, following the instructions for creating flower petals (see page 67).

2. Next, prepare the whiskers by cutting the fruit rope into six equal pieces. (Fig. 1)

3. Prepare the nose and mouth by cutting a mini marshmallows in half, and then one of the halves in half again. You will only use one marshmallow half and one marshmallow quarter for each bunny face. (Fig. 2 & 3)

5. Using a table knife, press a small slit into the center of one of the marshmallow quarters (but don't cut all of the way). This will be the bunny's mouth or teeth. (Fig. 4)

6. Insert one straw or cookie stick into each cookie, and coat with royal icing.

7. Using the chocolate chips, prepared mini marshmallows, and prepared fruit rope, create the bunny face.

8. Using toothpicks, secure two of the large marshmallow pieces (ears) to the top of the cookie.

FRUIT PIZZA COOKIES

What You Need

Fresh baked or store-bought cookies

Cream "Cheeze" Frosting *(see page 8)*

Strawberries

Blueberries

Egg slicer or knife

Chef Cookie Tip:

These cookies taste great with just about any kind of fruit. Get creative and experiment with different kinds of shapes and designs.

1

2

3

What To Do

1. Prepare strawberries by cutting out the stems and slicing with a clean egg slicer or knife, then set aside.

2. Frost cookies with cream "Cheeze" frosting *(see page 8)*.

3. Place strawberries on each cookie in a star shape. *(Fig 1 & 2)*.

4. Place three blueberries in the center of each star. *(Fig. 3)*

Fruit pizza cookies are a refreshing treat in the summertime heat

The cream "cheeze" frosting is a perfect compliment to the fruit and if you use store bought cookies for the base, you don't even have to turn on that hot oven!

ICE CREAM COOKIE SANDWICHES

What You Need

Two of your favorite cookies

Safe ice cream alternative

Safe sugar sprinkles

What To Do

1. Place a scoop of ice cream alternative on top of one cookie, then place another cookie on top of the ice cream.

2. Press flat and use a table knife to smooth edges, removing any excess ice cream.

3. Roll edges of cookie in sugar sprinkles.

4. Place on lined cookie sheet and store in freezer until ready to serve.

Did you know that cookie dough shakes first became popular in the 1990's?

I was at prime cookie baking age back then with no food allergies of my own and I couldn't figure out how restaurants could sell raw cookie dough without people getting sick from the raw eggs! Now that we are expert egg-less bakers, we know the answer to that question very well! There's no need for eggs in cookie dough! Next time you're whipping up some cookie dough, don't forget to save some in the freezer to mix into your next bowl of ice cream . . . yum!

90

Fall Cookies

Whether you're just heading back to school or you're getting ready for Halloween or Thanksgiving, these cookies are a fun way to celebrate!

BACK-TO-SCHOOL APPLE COOKIES

What You Need

Store bought or fresh baked cookies

Buttercream Frosting *(see page 7)*

Safe gummy worms

Safe food coloring

Green sugar sprinkles

Miniature marshmallows

Safe chocolate pieces

What To Do

1. Prepare marshmallows by cutting in half and pinching both ends to resemble a leaf shape.

2. Sprinkle sugar sprinkles over sticky part of marshmallow *(see instructions on page 63)*.

3. Stir red food coloring into frosting and spread on each cookie.

4. Use chocolate, marshmallow leaves, and worms to decorate each cookie.

What do you do to get ready to go back to school?

Do your parents help set up or renew a 504 plan for you and do you make sure your friends and teachers know how to help keep you safe in an emergency? Back to school time is a great time to get your epi prescriptions renewed and spread some allergy awareness messages at your school.

MONSTER MOUTH COOKIES

What You Need

Store bought or fresh baked cookies

Buttercream Frosting *(see page 7)*

Safe food coloring

Red sugar sprinkles

Miniature marshmallows

Large marshmallows

94

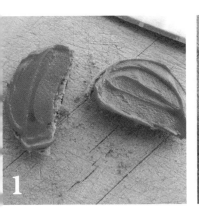 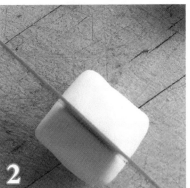   

What To Do

1. Gently saw each cookie in half. *(Fig. 1)*

2. Stir red food coloring into frosting and spread on each cookie half.

3. Prepare the monster tongue by cutting a large marshmallow in half and then cutting one end off of each half to create a tongue shape. *(Fig. 2 & 3)*

4. Sprinkle sugar sprinkles on the sticky sides of the tongue-shaped marshmallow piece. *(Fig. 4)*

5. Place on cookie half with mini marshmallows to resemble white teeth and a red tongue. *(Fig. 5)*

6. Top with remaining cookie half.

Chef Cookie Tip:

When cutting the cookies in half, use a dull knife to saw gentlly. Don't press hard on the cookie or it will crack and break where you don't want it too!

MUMMY COOKIES

What You Need

Black or brown cookies

Royal Icing *(see page 6)*

Candy pieces
(we used Skittles)

  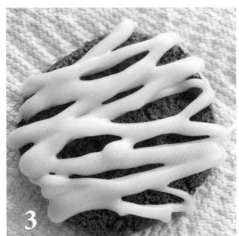 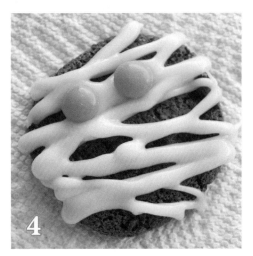

What To Do

1. Place icing in condiment bottle or decorator bag.

2. Moving slowly, draw lines with royal icing in a back and forth motion. *(Fig. 2)*

3. Repeat step two, but start from a different angle, crossing over existing lines diagonally. *(Fig. 3)*

4. Place two candies on the top third of the cookie to resemble eyes. *(Fig. 4)*

Chef Cookie Tip:

The speed you move the decorator bag or condiment bottle will determine the thickness of the royal icing it releases. For thicker lines, move slower. For thinner lines, move more quickly.

SPIDER COOKIES

What You Need

Soft cookies
  (black or brown)

Royal Icing
  (see page 6)

Safe fruit rope

Candy pieces
  (we used Skittles)

Toothpick

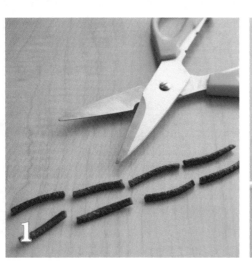   

What To Do

1. Prepare two fruit ropes by cutting each into four equal pieces. *(Fig. 1)*

2. On each soft cookie, poke four holes into each side of each cookie (for a total of eight holes). *(Fig. 2)*

3. Place fruit rope pieces into each hole to create spider legs. *(Fig. 3)*

4. Using royal icing, secure two candies on the top third of each cookie to resemble eyes. *(Fig. 4)*

EYEBALL COOKIES

What You Need

Two boxes chocolate cookies

8 oz. cream cheese alternative

1/2 c. safe yogurt

5 c. powdered sugar

Round gummy candies

Safe chocolate chips (mini)

Red food color marker

Plastic sandwich bag

What To Do

1. Place cookies in a sealed plastic bag and crush them with a spoon.

2. Mix crushed cookies with cream cheese alternative and roll into balls.

3. Place cookie balls on a wax paper lined cookie sheet and place in freezer for 10 minutes.

4. Meanwhile, have a grown up help you heat oven to 250 degrees F.

5. Blend yogurt and powdered sugar.

6. Place a cooling rack on a cookie sheet.

7. Remove cookie balls from freezer, coat in yogurt mixture, and place on cooling rack.

8. Place candies on top of each cookie.

9. Place one chocolate chip in the center of each gummy candy.

10. Turn off oven.

11. Place cookie sheet in warm oven for 3 to 4 hrs to set.

12. Remove cookie sheet and draw three lines on each cookie with a food marker to resemble blood shot eyes.

Chef Cookie Tip:

If you can't find a food marker that is safe for you, use the end of a sucker stick dipped in food coloring to draw the lines (see page 53).

In addition to the classic orange pumpkin color, try making this cookie with **teal frosting** to show your enthusiasm for the **Teal Pumpkin Project!**

PUMPKIN SUGAR COOKIE

What You Need

Store bought or fresh baked cookies

Buttercream Frosting
(see page 7)

Safe chocolate chips *(mini)*

Safe chocolate pieces

What are your Halloween trick-or-treating traditions?

Do you have a switch witch, great pumpkin, or goodie goblin that visits your house to take away unsafe candy on Halloween night? Maybe you just skip trick-or-treating all together and throw a fun party for the neighbors instead. How about a scavenger hunt for teal pumpkins ? Whatever you do, we hope you remember to stay safe and have fun !

What To Do

1. Stir orange food coloring into frosting and spread on each cookie.

2. Decorate with chocolate chips and chocolate pieces.

www.allergycookie.com

TURKEY COOKIES

What You Need

Store bought or fresh baked cookies

Sunflower seed butter or other nut butter alternative

Safe gummy candy *(we used DOTS)*

Safe chocolate chips

Coconut

Table knife

What To Do

1. Frost each cookie with sunflower seed butter or other nut butter alternative.

2. Have a grown up help you lightly toast the coconut and sprinkle over spread.

3. Prepare gummy candies by slicing into feather shapes.

4. Squeeze the end of one gummy candy to create a beak shape.

5. Cut one of the red candies into smaller pieces to create snoods.

6. Using chocolate chips and gummy candies, decorate your cookies.

Chef Cookie Tip:

Now that you've discovered a new medium for frosting cookies (sunflower seed butter), it's time to get creative and start inventing new cookies of your own! Try sunbutter & jelly cookie sandwiches or sunbutter puppy faces.

APPLE PIE COOKIES

What You Need

Pie crust dough

3 to 4 large apples

For the cinnamon sugar mixture:

1/4 c. sugar

2 t. cinnamon

TRY THIS PERFECT PIE CRUST:

https://www.allergycookie.com/the-perfect-pie-crust-gluten-free-vegan-top-8-free/

What To Do

1. Have a grown up help you preheat the oven to 350 degrees F.

2. Prepare the dough and divide into two equal pieces.

3. Roll each piece of dough between two pieces of wax paper and chill in freezer for 15 minutes.

4. While dough is chilling, have a grown up help you peel and chop the apples. *(Fig. 1)*

5. Remove one piece of dough from the freezer and gently peel away top piece of wax paper.

6. Top with half of cinnamon sugar mixture.

7. Top with apples. *(Fig. 2)*

8. Top with remaining cinnamon sugar mixture.

9. Remove remaining piece of dough from freezer and gently remove top layer of wax paper.

10. Slice into thin strips and place over apples in a criss cross pattern. *(Fig. 3 & 4)*

11. Cut into cookie shapes and place on prepared cookie sheet. *(Fig. 5)*

12. Bake at 350 degrees for 15 to 20 minutes.

Christmas Cookies

Santa will love these cute and tasty cookies on Christmas Eve and so will your family and friends when you make these for the next holiday party!

SANTA BELLY COOKIES

What You Need

Store bought or fresh baked cookies

Royal Icing
(see page 6)

Safe food coloring

Red sugar sprinkles

Wax paper

110

What To Do

1. Cut strips of wax paper, about the size you want the belt to be, and set aside.

2. Using safe food coloring, create red and black icing, leaving some icing white.

3. Frost the entire cookie in with red icing.

4. Place wax paper strips across the center of each cookie and sprinkle red sugar sprinkles over the cookie. *(Fig. 1 & 2)*

5. Slowly peel away the wax paper and let the cookie sit to dry and firm up.

6. Once the icing is firm, use a condiment bottle or decorator bag to fill in the belt area. *(Fig. 3)*

7. Promptly draw the belt buckle with white icing and let absorb/dry.

SANTA FACE COOKIES

What You Need

Store bought or fresh baked cookies

Buttercream Frosting
(see page 7)

Safe chocolate chips

Red sugar sprinkles

Red candy pieces
(we used Skittles)

Coconut

112

What To Do

1. Prepare a piece of wax paper, by tracing around one cookie to create a circle, then cut the circle out of the wax paper.

2. Frost each cookie with white frosting.

3. Place the circle piece of wax paper on each frosted cookie, one at a time, leaving 1/3 of the cookie exposed.

4. Sprinkle red sugar sprinkles on the exposed portion of the frosted cookie, then carefully remove the wax paper.

5. Remove the wax paper and sprinkle coconut on the bottom third of the cookie.

6. Place a little more coconut along the bottom edge of the hat, with a large clump on one side to resemble a pom pom.

7. Using the candy and chocolate chips, create Santa's face on the rest of the cookie.

Chef Cookie Tip:

Check out page 47 for a photo demonstrating this technique!

114

REINDEER COOKIES

What You Need

Store bought or fresh baked cookies

Sunflower seed butter or other nut butter alternative

Candy pieces *(we used Skittles)*

Safe chocolate chips (mini)

Wax paper

What To Do

1. Frost each cookie with sunflower seed butter or other nut butter alternative.

2. Melt some chocolate chips in the microwave by warming about 30 seconds at a time, stirring in between.

3. Place melted chocolate in a condiment bottle or decorator bag and use it to draw reindeer antlers on wax paper. Place in the freezer for 15 minutes to set.

4. In the meantime, use mini chips and candy pieces to create the reindeer faces.

5. Finally, carefully peel the antlers from wax paper and place on each cookie.

6. Using chocolate chips and gummy candies, decorate your cookies.

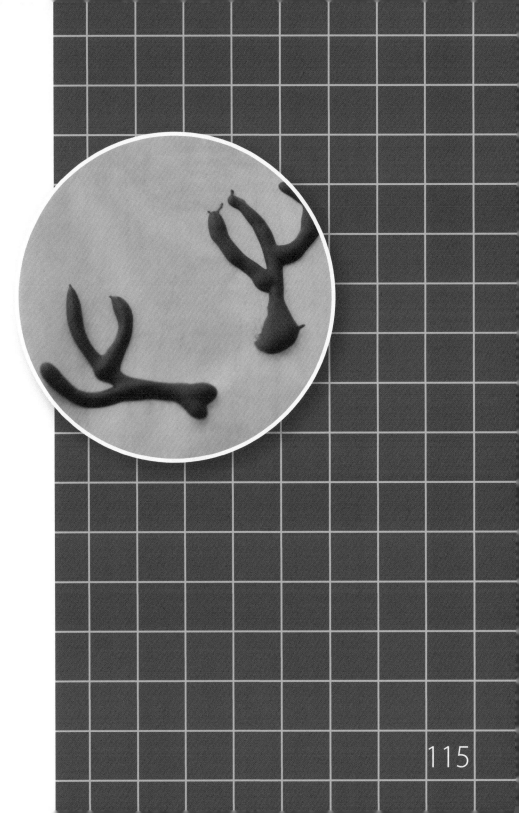

FILLED DRUM COOKIES

What You Need

Crisp or Crunchy cookies

Royal Icing *(see page 6)*

Safe food coloring

Candy pieces *(we used Skittles)*

Safe Jelly Beans or other soft candy

Small circle-shaped cookie cutter

Candy to fill drums (Surf Sweets featured)

Paper towel

Toothpicks

What To Do

1. Prepare your icing by dividing it into portions and using safe food coloring to create the colors you want.

2. Next, moisten a paper towel and squeeze to ring it out.

3. Wrap three cookies (one at a time) in the moist paper towel and microwave for about 20 to 30 seconds until soft.

4. Unwrap the cookie and use the cookie cutter to cut out the center and create a ring like shape.

5. Let the rings cool down and harden before continuing.

6. In the meantime, use royal icing to frost the top of an additional cookie (for the lid).

7. Using additional icing of a different color in a condiment bottle or decorator bag, create an outer border on the drum's lid.

8. Set aside and let the icing harden up.

9. Create the drum sticks by cutting a jelly bean in half and sticking each half on the ends of toothpicks.

10. Build a drum by placing a 5th, solid cookie in front of you and stacking each of the rings on top, one at a time, using icing to hold them in place.

11. Decorate the outside with additional royal icing and candies.

12. Fill the drum with candies and place the lid on top.

MARBLED HOLIDAY COOKIES

What You Need

Store bought or fresh baked cookies

Royal Icing
(see page 6)

Safe food coloring

Toothpick

What To Do

1. Divide the icing into thirds and create three different colors of icing using safe food coloring.

2. Using decorator bags, frost entire cookie with a base color *(white in this picture)*.

3. Promptly draw lines across the cookie in a pattern with the other colors. *(Fig. 1)*

4. Wiggle the cookie a little and wait a few seconds until the colors are blended but not firm.

5. Drag the end of a toothpick through each of the layers to create a marbled effect. *(Fig. 2)*

6. Let sit until firm and set.

Chef Cookie Tip:
For best results, let cookies set overnight before serving!

FRUITCAKE NO-BAKE COOKIES

What You Need

1 box Christmas DOTS Candies

3 c. cornflakes

1 1/2 c. Corn Chex cereal

1 1/2 c. Rice Chex cereal

1/4 c. coconut (optional)

4 ounces cream cheese alternative

3 T. safe butter alternative

1 1/4 c. sugar

1/2 c. safe milk alternative

1 t. vanilla

120

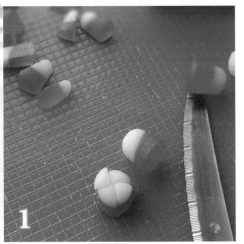

What To Do

1. Cut DOTS candies into fourths and set aside. *(Fig. 1)*

2. Seal Chex in plastic bag and crush with a spoon. *(Fig. 2)*

3. Mix with cornflakes & coconut.

4. Add cream cheese alternative (don't stir) and set aside. *(Fig. 3)*

5. In medium saucepan melt butter alternative, add milk alternative, sugar, and vanilla and bring to a rolling boil over medium high heat, stirring constantly.

6. Boil for one minute and remove from heat.

7. Stir into cereal mixture until well combined. *(Fig. 3)*

8. Stir in DOTS candies. *(Fig. 4)*

9. Drop onto wax paper coated cookie sheets and let cool until set.

SHARE WITH US!

Don't forget to show us how much fun you're having making safe cookies! Take pictures of your cookies in progress, take a selfie of yourself sampling the batter or eating your cookies, and take pictures of your finished product, too. Next, post your pictures on social media using the hashtag: #52Cookies and tag @AllergyCookie when you do! See you on the web!

f allergycookie

 allergycookie#

t @allergycookie

g+ +allergycookie

 allergycookie

Alphabetical Index

CPSIA information can be obtained at www.ICGtesting.com
Printed in the USA
BVIW121533210819
556235BV00031B/33